Live Loud, Love Loud

j.
iron word

For the dreamers,
the believers in love
and the hopeful souls.

Chapter

1

Truths

Love

Love does not live
by a watch or a
calendar, love does not
see skin tones or flaws,
love does not know hate
or violence, love does
not know giving up, but
love does know forever,
love does know
blindness and kindness,
love does know
forgiveness,
love does know hope.

j. iron word

Living

It is in the everyday
of life that living
happens, where memories
are made and love
lives.

j. iron word

Growth

Growth is not linear; it
is a maze of twists,
turns and regression.

Regression is full of
lessons learned,
forgotten and never
learned at all, but
always filled with
potential for progress.

Progress that sometimes
includes pain, pain that
sometimes includes
sorrow.

Sorrow is always a
delicate lesson, one
that rehashes memories
that we would often
rather forget.

However, in forgetting
we lose a part of who
we are, part of where
we came from and part

of our strength.

Growth is never
complete and is always
a work in progress.

j. iron word

Trust Issues

I have learned not to
trust my eyes, for they
only show me what I can
see.

j. iron word

"Start"

When we are born no
one is there to tell us
our lives have begun,
but we live anyway.
Somewhere along the
way we learn to be
careful and plan,
forgetting to press
"start" on living.

j. iron word

Better Together

You can give someone
the world and they
would still ask for the
moon, you could give
someone the moon and
they would still ask
for the sun, you could
give someone the sun
and they would still
ask for the stars, you
could give someone the
stars and they would
still ask for the
universe.

Whatever happened to it
being enough to simply
give yourself to
someone and working to
get the earth, the moon,
the sun, the stars and
the universe together?

j. iron word

Wisdom

Wisdom does not always
come from what you
know, but in having the
humility to learn from
others in what you do
not.

j. iron word

Somehow

Our physical appearance
is the smallest part of
us, but somehow it is
all that people see.

j. iron word

Hypocritical

People talk about
wanting to be accepted
for who they are, yet
talk about others for
being who they are.

j. iron word

Inside

We are all fractured
souls pretending to be
whole, when we are
really crumbling from
the inside out.

j. iron word

Stay Weird

Your weird
is someone's
perfect.

j. iron word

Long Enough

I have lived long
enough to know that
people break promises,
life is what you make
it and true love
exists.

j. iron word

Infinite

Love is not a word; it
is a series of never
ending actions.

j. iron word

Imperfection

If someone knows your
imperfections and they
love you wholly, they
do not think you are
perfect. Rather they
know you are not and
love you perfectly
anyway.

j. iron word

On

Be the kind
of soul whose
light doesn't have
an off switch.

j. iron word

Chosen

What I have come to
know is it is not where
we look for love that
matters the most or
even at all, but where
and when love chooses
to find us.

j. iron word

Wanted

We do not want to be
someone's afterthought.
We simply desire to be
someone's first, last
and every other
thought in-between.

j. iron word

Distance

Unconditional love will
take you further than
money ever will.

j. iron word

Stability

We do not want a love
on life support; give us
a stable love that
blows the doors off
of doubt.

j. iron word

The Lesson

The seconds, minutes,
hours, days, months and
years you spend with
another are never
wasted, but filled with
lessons learned and the
very best breakups
begin and end with new
heartbeats.

Beats that turn your
world right side up and
teach you the greatest
lesson of all,
unconditional
love.

j. iron word

Cracks

I can still find
you in the cracks
of my heart and
in the broken
memories we made
together.

And even in the
dreams that never
came true, where you
and I still exist.

j. iron word

Directions

Hearts can only be
pushed away for so
long, before they
begin to beat in the
direction of another.

j. iron word

Itself

Pianos do not play
themselves, hearts do
not break themselves,
but the sun will still
rise all by itself.

j. iron word

This Way

Maybe it is not about
finding the one that
turns your world upside
down, but in meeting
the one that keeps
your world right side
up.

j. iron word

Despite

The rarest flowers
stand out, because they
grow and thrive despite
their surroundings.

j. iron word

Love Math

We get tired of being
loved in fractions and
just want to be loved
whole for once.

j. iron word

Lost

Some people hide
who they really
are so much that
they lose themselves
in their own illusion.

j. iron word

Thanks

Sunday mornings
are for sleeping in,
sipping coffee and
self-reflection, for
thinking of all that
was accomplished in
the week before and
for planning the
days ahead, but
most importantly
for giving thanks.

j. iron word

Positively

Energy
is infectious, be
positively
viral.

j. iron word

Never

Never apologize
for not being the
"right one" for the
wrong person.

j. iron word

Someone

Be with someone
who helps you love
yourself more.

j. iron word

Reflections

Sometimes you just need
the right light shining
on you to see your true
reflection.

j. iron word

Straightforward

Life is straightforward
and so is love, but we
complicate them both
trying to make them
what they are not.

j. iron word

Your Winner

You do not have to be
for everyone, just be
made for one; a one that
will act as if life has
been won with you by
their side.

j. iron word

Irony

It is funny how someone
you thought you could
not live without can
become a stranger in a
blink and a stranger
could be the only one
you will never live
without.

j. iron word

The Cage

It is amazing how

r

i

b

s

can keep a
shattered heart
from falling out
for all the world
to see.

j. iron word

The Fall

Sometimes hearts do not
fall the way we want
them too, but what we
want and destiny are
two different things.

Let the hearts fall as
they may and in the end
you will see your
fallen heart right
beside your
"meant to be."

j. iron word

Void

I do not count
the days we talk,
but on those we
do not, I cannot
help but feel the
empty that you
leave.

The void that
ironically only
becomes filled
with thoughts
of you.

j. iron word

Refocus

How many yesterdays
have you spent your
todays on? How many
tomorrows have slipped
through your fingers
while you were focused
on what can never
change?

j. iron word

The Root

People are
not born bitter;
they are "loved"
into it.

j. iron word

Your Volume

Sometimes you
have to turn down
the speakers of the
voices of others and
turn up the volume
of yours.

j. iron word

Power

The most loyal people
can hurt you, the most
honest lie, but you
have the greatest
power of all, that
of forgiveness.

To forgive however
does not always mean
allowing that person
back in your life, but
it does mean you can
let go and move on.

j. iron word

Chaotic Insanity

The insanity that lives
within the world knows
no boundaries, just as
the chaos that reigns
within our hearts.

j. iron word

Tales

The most perfect
love stories are not
fairytales they are
resilient tales.

j. iron word

An Introduction

Two lost hearts
without direction
are nothing more
than a hello away
from forever.

j. iron word

Twisted

Tongues
were meant
to taste and
be tasted.

j. iron word

Chapter

2

Being
Human

Something Human

The human experience
is often the same, but
if we do not vocalize
those experiences we
will never make the
connection that we
are a part of
something bigger
than ourselves,
something
human.

j. iron word

Understood

I would rather
be forever alone,
than be forever
misunderstood.

j. iron word

Still

I feel love
for every human
I have ever loved.

Even if it has been
years it still exists
in the far corners
of my heart.

j. iron word

Me

Growing up,
I was told I
could be anything
I wanted to be,
except the me
I was growing
into being.

j. iron word

Enlightenment

I have learned
more in the darkness
of my life, than in
the light of any
classroom.

j. iron word

What If?

What if my heart
stopped, would my
soul cease to exist
or would it still
live by the same
rhythm and beat
it has always
lived by?

j. iron word

Walls

Maybe our
walls exist
not to keep
people out,
but to stop
ourselves
from loving
someone who
will not love
us back.

j. iron word

Humanity

Maybe we are
only as strong
as the hands
helping those
in need.

j. iron word

Forward

I do not
burn bridges,
I demolish them,
going back is not
of interest to me,
I only strive to
move forward.

j. iron word

Temporary

In a world where
everything is treated
as temporary, I have
gotten good at
goodbyes.

j. iron word

My Melody

Music often
accompanies me,
my thoughts,
my moods,
my silence.

j. iron word

My Best

My best days will
never be behind me,
as long as my heart
is capable of loving,
my mind is capable of
thinking and my soul is
capable of illuminating.

j. iron word

Beneath

What lies beneath,
can never be measured
by a scale, nor be owned
by another, has thoughts
that never end and ideas
that are just beginning.

What lies beneath,
is capable of
unimaginable dreams
and a heart that loves
without conditions.

What lies beneath you
ask?

You do.

j. iron word

Complex Simplicity

You are simple in your
desires but complex as a
whole. You are focused
and driven, but still
crave to be loved and
cared for. Not because
you cannot care for
yourself, rather it
would be nice to know
that someone is there
that you can count on
as much as yourself.

j. iron word

Fly

I dream
therefore
I fly.

I fly
therefore
I live.

j. iron word

"Good enough"

I used to want to be
"good enough" to be
accepted. I craved it,
but the harder I tried
the more I seemed to be
on the outside looking
in. This is when I
realized that it wasn't
myself that was on the
outside, it was those
who failed to get to
know me for who I was.
Those who judged me for
what I looked like or
where I came from
rather than for the
human behind the skin.
I no longer have the
same desire to be "good
enough," because I know
it is not me who has
the problem. It is those
who live life with
judgment in their eyes.

j. iron word

Self

I have never been
understood by many,
but I do not need to be;
as long as I have the
understanding of self.

j. iron word

Hello

I will never say
goodbye to yesterday,
for I am me because of
where I have been.

But in saying hello
to my tomorrow, I am
introducing myself to
the me I was intended
to be.

j. iron word

Sleeves

I have always worn
my heart on my sleeve.
In doing so I have been
hurt enough to make
pain forever be a part
of my heart, but I still
love despite it, because
I know a love that
never leaves is worth
all the hurt I have
ever known.

j. iron word

Connection

One of my favorite
things about us, is
being able to pick
up where we left off.

No matter the time
between us, it is almost
as if we have been
there all along.

j. iron word

Unbridled

I miss you
in my mouth
and beneath
my tongue.

The taste of you
dripping from my
lips and fingertips.

The sounds of
your moans and
your nails in
my skin.

I miss being in
complete control
while having no
control.

j. iron word

I Thought

While I know
not every person
in your life is
meant to be
forever.

I thought you
would be different.
I thought you would
be there, I thought
you would be here,
with me.

j. iron word

Fragile

There is a
broken inside
of me that I hide
within my strength,
but my heart is just
as fragile as the day
it was first broken.

j. iron word

Space

There is a place
in the middle of the
ocean with no name and
no one to hear even the
loudest of screams.

Sometimes I go there in
my mind, far away from
the concrete, the lights
and the sounds of the
voices of those who
know what's "best" for
me.

While I am there I do
not worry of losing
myself in the depths
of solitude, but
finding myself.

j. iron word

Empty

I have always
been one to hold
on for too long, not
realizing until it's too
late that I am alone
and holding on to
nothing more than
empty promises.

j. iron word

The Keepers

I have learned
not to count the
goodbyes of those
who have left my
life, but only the
hellos of those
who have stayed.

j. iron word

Human

The jaded in me
tells me not to feel,
but the human in me
just cannot help it.

Life can be cruel and
some heartbreaks may
never mend, but I live
and breathe knowing
love can be the next
heartbeat away.

j. iron word

Always

I will always look for
you in a crowd of
strangers.

I will always dream of
you long past tomorrow,
just like it was
yesterday.

There will always be a
song that takes me back
to a time or a place
where you and I shared
a memory.

There will always be a
part of my day that I
will think of you and
want to share.

A part of me will
always be yours, no
matter where life takes
me.
j. iron word

The Unseen

Maybe you cannot see
the darkness within me,
a darkness that is
trying to take over my
body.

A darkness that is
trying to take away
everything I am and
everything that I have.

A darkness that is
trying
to take me away from
everyone
that loves me.

But regardless of what
you
can or cannot see, what
I know
for certain is that it
cannot see
that I am me.

A me that has a will to
live, a me that has the
will to survive, a me
that has a will to see a
thousand more sunsets
beside those that are
loved by me.

A me that will beat
this darkness with all
the light
within me.

j. iron word

Chapter

3

Her

Her

When asked
the color of
love all he said
was, "Her."

j. iron word

Unbreakable

There is a confidence
in her silence that can
only be described as
unbreakable and a strong
in her stature that is
self-made, and there is
nothing more powerful
than an unbreakable
self-made woman.

j. iron word

Delicate Strength

Fragile comes in
many forms and she
is the most delicate
thing that has ever
been broken, but is
now the strongest
because of it.

j. iron word

She is Love

She is a flashback
to everything that
love is and everything
that love should be,
she's... well she is
everything.

j. iron word

"It"

Maybe it's the sweet in
her sass or the shake
in her ass, but one
thing's for sure she's
got that "it" that could
shine on the sun and a
flare that could
outshoot the stars.

j. iron word

Caught

When she smiles because
of her laugh, she has a
way of catching you in
between heartbeats, a
way of catching you.

j. iron word

Lips

Her parted lips
only remind me
of two separated
souls, living,
breathing and
craving a passion
to call home.

j. iron word

Wild Thing

She's not a
fan of roses, but
she is of all things
wild; wildflowers,
living and love to
name a few.

It is in those things
that she sees herself
most in and it is in
those things that she
flourishes.

j. iron word

Rainbow

She's the gunpowder
in a firework that
lights up the sky,
with a personality
that holds a rainbow
of colors for those
brave enough to play
with her fire.

j. iron word

Soulgenic

She is so
much more than
beauty on camera,
her soulful existence
thrives like oxygen
in a garden.

j. iron word

She can

Laugh with the
best of them, live
unlike the rest of
them and love like
it's never been done
before.

j. iron word

The One and Only

She is nothing you
would expect her to
be, but everything
she dreamt of being.

An old soul in a
digital world, an
anchor over troubled
water, the kind of
woman you love
until your last
breath.

j. iron word

Wanted

She's the strong
and quiet type and
she's not impressed
with loud and flashy.

She respects those
like her, someone who
works without needing
a single approval from
anyone but themselves.

j. iron word

Page Turner

And sometimes
she smiles despite
the pain, as she
turns the page to
a new tomorrow.

j. iron word

Completely Beautiful

She doesn't know the
meaning of shallow and
humble is all she is.

She is blind to the
depth of her beauty,
that is complete with
a shimmering heart,
mind and soul.

j. iron word

Darkness

Her eyes tell
a truth of a beautiful
mind and a simple but
seemingly difficult
wish, that she can be
seen for exactly who
she is while standing
in complete darkness.

j. iron word

Effortless

She may be
Small in stature,
but she carries
love effortlessly.

j. iron word

Easy

She made it
look easy, that thing
called life. Maybe it
was the pep in her step
or the smile on her
face, but whatever it
was, she owned it.

j. iron word

Timing

While she has never
been written about, it
is just a matter of
time, because she is
living poetry.

j. iron word

Nameless

She will never be the
girl with no name. She
will be the one you
cannot forget, the one
you saw and left your
heart forever in awe.
The one you will wonder
what could have been
had you just said hello.

j. iron word

Illuminate

She is different,
because she does not
wish for the light to
shine on her, but for
the light to shine
brightly on souls that
illuminate her.

j. iron word

Legacy

She lived a life she
was proud of, one she
lead with her heart,
one she hoped would
leave a legacy of love.

j. iron word

Human

She is not a doll
made of plastic, she
is a mind and soul that
needs to breathe just as
the beauty that rests
on her bones.

j. iron word

Inside

As she grew tired
of the tears, her
cheeks began to dry
and her new began to
grow, from the inside
out.

j. iron word

First and Last

His first mistake was
taking her for granted;
his last, was thinking
she could not live
without him.

j. iron word

Sunflower

She's a sunflower
effortlessly standing
out from the rest.

Her petals reach for
the sky in the light of
day, but still stands
tall in darkness.

Her very existence
gives life to all those
around her.

j. iron word

Lunar Art

She has an incomparable
dopeness to her unlike
anything you have ever
seen before; she is
graffiti on the moon.

j. iron word

Lost

One look at her
direction and you are
lost at sea, in a sea of
thoughts, in a sea of
emotions, in the sea of
her existence...

j. iron word

Rainy Sunday

She is a rainy
Sunday afternoon with
potential for passion,
music and relaxation at
any moment.

j. iron word

Wordless

They say a picture is
worth a thousand words,
but one look at hers
and you are left
without any.

j. iron word

Feminine Freedom

There is a
Freedom she only
finds in the curves
of her femininity.

j. iron word

Conquered

He took her
by the hand and
showed her the world
that was hers to be had.
The one that was hers
for the making, and he
stood silently behind
her as she conquered
all of her hearts
desires.

j. iron word

Wolf Lessons

She did not need
to be raised by wolves
to become savage, just
"loved" by the wrong
people.

j. iron word

Fearless

She is fearless,
but maybe that is
why she is living
a life worthy of
reliving, while
others are busy
slowly dying.

j. iron word

Genes

She's the type of
fierce that is hard to
follow and impossible
to replace.

Flawlessly rocking
what she was born with
the only way she knows,
her own.

j. iron word

Glimpse

One glimpse of her
and your heart and
mind are left without
or reason, but life
waits on no man and
neither does her love.

j. iron word

Cosmo Colored Dreams

She's the kind of
beautiful you spend
your lifetime dreaming
about.

The kind of intelligent
that leaves your mind
thinking long after
you've exchanged words
and the kind of sexy
that makes you bite
your lip leaving it
blood red.

j. iron word

The Why

It is not so much
the color or the
type of flower that
she cares for, as
much as why they
are given to her.

j. iron word

New Chapter

She did not see
motherhood as an
ending to her life,
but as a beginning
to a new chapter titled
"Unconditional Love."

j. iron word

Power

Her superpower
came in the form of
empowering herself.

Once she realized she
was unstoppable all
alone, the world was
hers.

j. iron word

Muse

While she oozes sexy
from her hips, lips and
fingertips. It's the
curve of her heart and
mind that makes her a
creature of myth.

She loves and lives
with a passion that can
only be described as all
or nothing, paired with
a mind that craves soul
filling letters and
words from a poetic
heartbeat that mirrors
her own.

She is a living and
breathing muse, a soul
who needs no
introduction to life or
love.

j. iron word

Chapter

4

Love

Answered

It was in the way he
looked at her, like she
was the answer to all
of his prayers and it
was in that very same
moment that he knew
there was a God.

j. iron word

Cemented

Rather than ask
who broke her heart,
he loved her, and while
he could not change the
past.

He could do everything
in his power to make
sure their future was
cemented in love.

j. iron word

Insane Beauty

It's beautifully
insane how perfectly
compatible we are with
one another, even in
the ways that made us
completely incompatible
with others.

j. iron word

Life

"I just want to life
with you," he said.

"Don't you mean live?"
She replied.

"No I mean life,
experiencing and living
all the things that two
people can share when
they spend a lifetime
together," he answered.

j. iron word

Safe

I once told myself
that I would never love
again and I locked my
heart and threw away
the key.

Until one day I heard
something on the other
side of the self-made
walls that had become
my "safe place," that of
another heart. Peeking
over my walls I saw a
soul that was more
beautiful than anything
I had ever seen.

One that surpasses
a sunrise on the
ocean's waves and
only compares to
the moonlight in
their eyes. In that
moment I found the
safest place of them
all, their arms.

Engulfed

I waited at the foot
of your sea for your
love to come and
engulf me.

Now I find
myself right-side
up while drowning in
your love and there
is nowhere else I
would rather be
than wrapped up
in the chaos of
your waves.

j. iron word

Falling

To the brink
we push and push,
rooted deeply in
unhinged passion.

Our chests
beating from
the inside out,
we let go.

Falling
Over the edge
we land nowhere,
but feeling
everything
together.

j. iron word

My Choice

You did not tell me to
say hello, but I did
anyway.

You did not tell me to
care, but I did anyway.

You did not tell me to
keep in touch, but I did
anyway.

You did not tell me to
be there, but I was
anyway.

You did not tell me to
get my hopes up, but I
did anyway.

You did not tell me to
fall in love, but I did
anyway.

You did not tell me to
wait, but I will anyway.

Madness

With you I am
not afraid to show
you my broken, because
I know you will love
me anyway and help
me make sense of the
madness that resides
within my soul.

j. iron word

Pieces

I promise
to keep your pieces
together when you fall
and love you to pieces
when you are
together.

j. iron word

Posted

I posted letters
of love with the hope
that they would help
you find your way to
me. Now I write them
with the hope that you
will never lose your
way again.

j. iron word

I am Here

Uncertainty is a
tough tight rope to
walk alone, but I am
here standing on the
other side extending
myself to you.

j. iron word

I can

I can be your brain
when yours is tired,
your heart when yours
is hurting and your
arms when you need
holding.

j. iron word

Up

We lift each other
up even when we are
both down, but that's
just part of the
unconditional in
our love.

j. iron word

Completely

I love you in a way you
have never been loved,
I am not saying I love
you better or worse,
but I do love you
completely.

j. iron word

My Way

Telling me not
to care is like
telling me not
to breathe.

Unless you want
to love a still heart,
let me love you the
only way I know how,
my way.

j. iron word

Something Else

I have always lived
life a certain way.
Thinking it was the
only way, but something
else came into it
showing me what life
could and should be.

That something else was
you and you opened my
eyes to what love is.

Love, something else
entirely different from
what I had ever
experienced before and
for the first time ever
my heart placed a you
before me.

And rather than tell
you to "trust me," I am
going to ask you to do
something else, to watch
me, the me that now
exists because of you.

141

It is now my turn to
show you what love is
and it is going to be
something else,
something more,
something amazing.

j. iron word

Complete

I love the cracks
that make your whole
and I love the whole
that you make my
broken.

j. iron word

Leveling

When my tub is
overflowing only
you can climb in
with me and level
the waters.

j. iron word

Life Artist

I will never be
able to put pencil
to paper and sketch it
to life, but I will do
everything within my
power to give you a
life worth living and
loving over and over
again.

j. iron word

Cherished

She doesn't understand
why I call her Queen,
but I don't understand
why she has not been
cherished as one.

j. iron word

Worthy

I love you more than
me and that is not to
say that I do not love
me, because I do. I just
love the you that lives
within your bones, the
soul that calls your
existence home and the
mind that lives behind
your thoughts enough to
know you're worthy of
such a love.

j. iron word

Maybe It's

We naturally
gravitate to
one another,
maybe it's
our chemistry,
maybe it's
our connection,
maybe it's
our history,
or maybe it's as
simple as we are
meant to be.

j. iron word

Just a Little

Throughout my nights,
days and dreams you
accompany me, you are
never too far from my
heart and mind. I just
hope you feel me even
just a little, from time
to time.

j. iron word

Her Omega

I am not the first man
to love her and I sure
as hell won't be the
last, but I hope to God
I am the last she loves
back.

j. iron word

You are

You are the water in
the vase, the green in
the stem and the color
in the petals. Your
beauty has always been
there and will continue
to be and if you let me
I will be the table you
rest upon.

j. iron word

Everything

Everything that
we are together is all
that I crave when we
are apart and all that
we are, is all that I
ever want to be,
forever.

j. iron word

Red

It was the red in
the wine or the pink
in her lips, but the
line between love and
lust became just as
blurred as a street
light after 2 a.m.

But I didn't worry
looking back, for my
eyes were too busy
being wide shut.

j. iron word

The Intrigue

Maybe it's the beauty
of the organized chaos
in your mind that
keeps me coming back
for more, the intrigue
of your next thought,
your next brush with
insanity.

j. iron word

Undying

I am not afraid of
dying, but I am afraid
of leaving you here
without me. Without you
knowing that even if
that day comes, I will
still be here as I am
today, your shadow's
heartbeat.

j. iron word

Honey

As my eyes grow
heavy and I drift off
to dream, my smile still
shines brightly knowing
that a soul as sweet as
honey lives and
breathes in you.

j. iron word

11:59

Tomorrow is only a few
heartbeats away, but I
do not want to spend it
dreaming, when we have
this very second where
we can love and live
out our dreams
together.

j. iron word

Intensity

My effort for you
and in us does not
stop when we are not
together. If anything,
it intensifies working
harder, living loudly
and loving you
completely.

j. iron word

Addicted

People see us
and often wonder what
we are on, but little
do they know it is as
simple as the same
wavelength.

j. iron word

Gratitude

I am thankful for
every person that let
you go, in doing so they
led you right to me.

j. iron word

Together

We could never just
be friends when we are
together, and we could
never just be strangers.

We could only be what
we were always meant
to be, together.

j. iron word

Found

"I'm home," he said.

"I know," she replied,
as she pulled him to
her.

j. iron word

Why?

She asked him why he
loved her?

And he asked her why
did she breathe?

She replied, "To live."

"Me too,"
he said.

j. iron word

We Can

Maybe you and I will
never be nothing more
than flawed, but that
does not mean we cannot
love each other as
perfectly as we can.

j. iron word

On Repeat

Time may disappear
when we are together,
but our memories live
over and over again.

j. iron word

Color

Long before there
was a you or an us, I
had hope that I would
find you.

Somehow through
the twists and turns
of life I landed in a
love that was as vivid
and colorful as the
reflection of the
world through
your eyes.

j. iron word

Inspiration

Even on the days
that you feel less
than your best, you
still inspire all
the love within
me.

j. iron word

Earned

Trust is the
hardest thing to
earn and the easiest
to lose, but I would
rather spend my life
earning and keeping
yours, than to lose
you in a moment of
insecurity.

j. iron word

Patched

I tried to forgive
myself, and I came up
short, but you forgave
me and loved us enough
to patch my hearts
flaws.

j. iron word

Shadow

There is something
about the way light
reflects off of you
and the shadows your
body casts, that makes
me want to memorize
every inch of your
darkness and light.

j. iron word

Love Anarchy

We share a wild love,
one that draws outside
the lines.

One that makes its own
rules and redefines the
word "love" itself.

j. iron word

The Dance

Little did she know
that in her being
"okay" with being her,
he was "okay" with
being him, because he
knew he was not alone
for as long as her feet
danced across from his
in this thing called
life.

j. iron word

Melted

There's something
about our naked
conversations draped
only in one another's
skin, that melts our
souls together in a
way that forever is
our only future.

j. iron word

Timeless

One day my
body will age,
my skin will loosen
and become spotted,
my muscles will weaken,
my fine lines will turn
into wrinkles, my hair
will fade to gray,
my young will turn to
old, but all will not be
lost as my naive will
turn wise and my love
for you will grow
ever more green.

j. iron word

Time

He gave her time;
time to love her,
time to appreciate her
and time to remind her
she was irreplaceable.

j. iron word

Spoken

I am more afraid
of letting go, than of
holding on and ending
broken, but before that
day comes I promise to
have spoken all my
hearts undying
devotion.

j. iron word

Subconscious Hopes

I cannot help what I
dream and while I know
they are just dreams,
they keep me going even
if they never come
true.

j. iron word

Numbers

He had the strength of
empowerment, strength
that could not be
measured with
weights, but in
worlds.

Specifically the
stresses in her
world, the stronger
she was, the stronger
he became.

He knew there was
strength in numbers
and there was no
greater number
than their two
souls together.

j. iron word

11:11

Always reminds me
of you and I.

11 our parallel, but
separate lives before
our existence:

11 our time side by
side together since.

j. iron word

The Us Frequency

You and I vibe
at a different level;
our own and that
is why we have
conversations that
never end. Ones that
somehow seem to be
just beginning, even
after hours on
end.

j. iron word

Soulful Love

As the seconds turn
into years and our
faint lines turn into
aged impressions, I will
love you.

Although you are the
most beautiful human I
have ever seen, I see
you from the inside out,
and for this reason my
attraction and desire
for you will only
intensify.

I do not merely make
love to your body, but
to your soul.

j. iron word

Given

Your human is what you
call me and your human
is what I always want
to be.

The human on the other
end of the line, the
human beside you, the
human there on the good
days and the bad, the
human you call home.

Your human is what you
call me and your human
is what I always want
to be.

Not because you bought
me, but because I gave
myself to you, freely,
willingly, body and
soul.

j. iron word

The Race

There will never be
enough hours in the
day to love you or
enough beats in my
heart to show you how
deep my love for you
runs, but I will spend
every second I have
left on this blue
marble racing against
the clock to align the
stars to make sure you
know that I do.

j. iron word

Open Arms

From the beginning of
us, nothing could keep
us apart.

While distance tried, it
wasn't enough to keep
us from falling.

Even when our minds
attempted to intervene,
our hearts did not
listen and continued
beating as one.

But as time went on our
connection could not
fill the

gap between our
separate lives, needing
more we fell apart.

Getting back up I am
now standing taller
than ever and I am here
to remind you that some
bonds can never be
broken and some wishes
come true.

While I would like
to spend the rest of my
life with you by my
side; I will spend the
rest of my life waiting,
with open arms.

Soul Film

When I look back at the
story of us, I see
flashbacks of the
memories my heart and
mind deemed as
unforgettable.

However I cannot help
but wonder what our
story would look, sound
and feel like if we
combined our memories
together and played
them on a screen that
only our souls could
see; the images and
snippets that make us
who we are as pair.

Most of all I would
look forward to seeing
the best part side by
side, the never-ending
part.

Unwavering

"Thank you for the
time of my life."
He whispered as he
squeezed her hand
already in his.

"It was my pleasure"
she said, as a tear
ran down her cheek.

Who knew a lifetime
together could pass
so quickly, they
thought and their
hearts raced as fast as
the day they
first met.

j. iron word

Index

Chapter 1
Truths

Chapter 2
Being Human

Chapter 3
Her

Chapter 4
Love

9 780692 072639

Printed in March 2021
by Rotomail Italia S.p.A., Vignate (MI) - Italy